Leo Tolstoy's

War and Peace Companion

*Includes Study Guide, Historical Context,
Biography, and Character Index*

BookCaps™ Study Guides

www.bookcaps.com

Cover Image © Jevgenijs Fjodorovs - Fotolia.com

Table of Contents

About the Author

Leo Nicolaevich Tolstoy was born in 1828, in an upper-class family. He attended the University of Kazan in 1844. As a young man, he had an active social life. In 1852, he joined the army and was posted along the border of Georgia, where he occasionally participated in expeditions against the Chechenians. He began to travel abroad in 1857, but by then he was a famous writer.

He was married to Sonya Andreyevna Bers, and she helped him manage his country estate and edit his books. During the years that his family was growing, he wrote War and Peace, as well as Anna Karenina.

While he was writing Anna Karenina, he suffered a major crisis, which lead to his conversion. Afterward, he became more and more obsessed with his quest for the ultimate truth of human existence. These philosophies divided him from his family, but they also often show up in his writing.

Historical Background

In War and Peace, Tolstoy writes about an actual war, the Patriotic War of 1812, which is not to be confused with the war between the US and Britain in the same year.

Here's the rundown of this war, which was between France and Russia. Napoleon marched into Russia in June, crossing the Neman River. After several smaller battles and fights, the French army ended up in Borodino, right outside of Moscow. This was the bloodiest battle in Napoleon's career. Even though France technically won the battle of Borodino, they lost so many men that, after they'd captured Moscow, they were unable to continue in Russia. The Russian army, on the other hand, grew in strength from new recruits, and proceeded to chase and slaughter any fragments of the French army.

Even though Tolstoy was not alive yet to see this war, which the Russians call the Patriotic War of 1812, he did have experience with warfare, having both served as a soldier and a war correspondent. As a journalist, he reported on horrific battlefield scenes, painting some of the world's first realistic word pictures of the tragedy of war.

So when we read War and Peace, we want to keep two things in mind. First, this was a real war, and much of the events are very accurate historically. Kutuzov, Alexander, and Napoleon were all real people. In fact, War and Peace was one of the first books to combine reality with fiction. Tolstoy portrayed historic figures alongside fictional characters of his novel, blending two genres to make something new. So when you read of the fighting and bloodshed, remember that all that really happened.

The Second thing to keep in mind about War and Peace is that many of the events (or kinds of events) in the book were taken from Tolstoy's personal experience. He did see horrific battles as both a soldier and journalist. He was very familiar with Russian aristocracy because he grew up in that kind of environment. The real human issues Tolstoy writes about are real for him, and that should make them even more real for us.

Overall Plot

War and Peace really is a monster of a novel, written in 15 separate books and 2 epilogues. Let's look at each book individually to see what it's about.

BOOK I

This book basically introduces the main characters. We first see a party at Anna Pavlovna's house and meet some important people. Then we jump over to a celebration at the Rostov's home. Finally, we go to Old Count Bezuhov's home, where he dies, leaving all his wealth and title to his illegitimate son, Pierre.

BOOK II

Both Nikolai Rostov and Prince Andrei get their first taste of war against the French. While they had ideas of grandeur and glory in battle, those dreams were quickly crushed by the reality of war. Nikolai accepts that he is nothing by a cog in the machine, and not a war hero. Andrei decides not to work as an administrator, choosing instead to fight as a common soldier.

BOOK III

Back home, Pierre marries Helene, even though he doesn't want to at first. Anatole courts Marya, but she turns him down. Andrei is nearly wounded in battle, and he is even treated by the French. He sees Napoleon before being let go. Everyone at home thinks he's dead and is surprised when he shows up in one piece.

BOOK IV

Nikolai is home on leave, and he ignores his one-time sweetheart Sonya. Pierre nearly kills a man in a duel. Liza, Andrei's wife, dies giving birth to their son, which leaves him feeling profound guilt. Nikolai gambles his way into a great debt to Anatole, which his family struggles to pay back.

BOOK V

Separating from his wife, Pierre joins the Masons to find what is good and right. He finds hope in their teachings. He and Nikolai have a conversation about some of those teachings, and Andrei seems to take to them, as well. Nikolai's friend, Denisov, faces court martial for stealing food form his starving men. Nikolai goes directly to the Emperor to request a pardon, but Alexander refuses.

BOOK VI

Andrei works to reform life and government, but then he falls in love with Natasha and suddenly reforming has lost its charm. Pierre begins to lose faith in the beliefs of the Freemasons. Marya is being constantly frustrated by her increasingly senile father. The Rostovs' financial situations gets worse as they go deeper into debt.

BOOK VII

This book is all about saying goodbye to youth and facing adult life. The Rostovs spend time as a happy family together, in a wolf hunt and sleigh ride. Natasha misses Andrei, who has promised to marry her. But the family seems close and happy, even though they are nearly bankrupt.

BOOK VIII

Natasha sees city life for the first time, and because she is growing into a beautiful young woman, many from the city take notice of her. Anatole especially forms a plot to trick her into giving her innocence to him, and she is nearly abducted by him. Afterward, she has a complete breakdown, and Pierre is there to comfort her.

BOOK IX

The full-on war between France and Russia begins as Napoleon invades. Andrei, having left Natasha behind, give himself over to serving in his regiment. Nikolai takes a French prisoner and is given a decoration. Petya joins the army, and even Pierre is caught up in a patriotic spirit. Natasha begins to recover from her traumatic experience with Anatole.

BOOK X

The French march on, deeper into Russian territory. After Marya and Andrei's father dies, she moves the household into Moscow, but the French are still getting closer to that city. Nikolai rides in and saves Marya from a dangerous situation, allowing her to flee Moscow just before the French arrive. They seem to fall in love at first sight. The bloody battle of Borodino takes many live, but it's a turning point, because afterward Russia begins to win the war.

BOOK XI

Massive events, according to Tolstoy, are the result of endless smaller events, many of which cannot be predicted. He outlines the demise of Moscow, the abandoning of the city, the arrival of Napoleon and the French Army, the looting and burning of the city, even the last stand by a drunk militia, started by the well-intentioned governor of the city.

BOOK XII

After the taking of Moscow, Nikolai and Marya meet again. Andrei has been injured and is expected to die, so Marya travels to where the Rostovs are. There, Natasha is taking care of her beloved. Meanwhile, Pierre has been captured in Moscow and is nearly executed by the French.

BOOK XIII

The French retreat, the Russians following after, capturing or slaughtering as many enemy soldiers as possible. Pierre, still a prisoner of the French, finds freedom and happiness, despite his plight.

BOOK XIV

Denisov and Dolokhov are leading guerilla attacks against the Russians. Petya, now a young officer in the army, wants to fight with them. Petya is killed right away, shot in the head. In the attack, however, Pierre is released from captivity.

BOOK XV

Andrei has died and the war is over. Natasha must stop her mourning to comfort her mother, who has now learned that her son, Petya, has died. Marya must help in household responsibilities, now that both her father and brother are dead. There is lover between Pierre and Natasha, just as there is love between Nikolai and Marya. Kutuzov, meanwhile, retires from military life.

FIRST EPILOGUE

Tolstoy tells what happens to some of the characters. Marya and Nikolai marry and have children, as do Pierre and Natasha. They are happy together, living good live, although they still have each their faults. Andrei's son is growing up, and he wants to be like Pierre (his personal hero) and his father.

SECOND EPILOGUE

Tolstoy ends the novel with a long philosophical essay on the meaning of truth in history and free will.

Characters

Here are the Main Characters of War and Peace, organized by family. This is probably the best way to remember them. Also, some pronunciation tips are included by the hardest names. When it comes to pronunciation, however, don't stress too much. Remember that in Russian, these names weren't even originally spelled with the English alphabet, so their true pronunciation includes sounds that don't exist in English. (Also, depending on the translation you read, the names might be spelled differently. Andrei might be Andrey, for example, or Liza might be Lisa. We tried to stay with one spelling all the way through.)

The Bolkonsky (bowl-CONE-skii) Family

Prince Bolkonsky

From an honorable family in Russia, this is Andrey and Marya's father. He's an old man at the beginning of the book, and he actually dies by the end. He loves order and learning.

Andrei (an-DREY)

He is heir of his father's estate. He is an intellectual. He treats his wife badly at the beginning of the novel, but after he death, he goes through some radical changes.

Marya (MAR-ya)

Andrei's sister, Marya faithfully raises Andrei's son after Liza's death. She also stays with her father, even when he makes her feel horrible all the time. She is very religious and loyal to a fault.

Other, less common characters in this family include: Liza, Andrei's wife who dies giving birth to their only child; Andrei's son, named Nikolushka and later Nikolinka; Madamoiselle Bourienne, a Frenchwoman that lives with the family, a little like a servant.

The Bezuhov (*beh-ZOO-hof*) Family

Count Bezuhov

An old man who, when about to die, leaves all his riches to his illegitimate son, Pierre.

Pierre

A major hero of the novel. He inherits a vast estate, even when he would have never expected to. He's very intellectual. He's basically coerced into marrying a beautiful but unfaithful wife. He leaves her and becomes a Mason. He's progress through the novel illustrates Tolstoy's philosophies.

The Rostov (*rus-TOHF*) Family

The Rostovs are by far the most functional and close-knit family in the novel. Even when they go through horrible financial circumstances, they manages to be happy and lean on each other for support.

Count Rostov

Nikolai and Natasha's father, a loving and good-natured man.

Countess Rostov

The count's wife, who is a typical noblewoman of the time. She wants the best for her children, and she is always trying to protect them.

Natasha

A major heroine of the novel, Natasha begins as a young girl but then grows into a beautiful young woman. She is notably happy and positive about things in life, which is probably why she is hurt so bad by Anatole's manipulations.

Nikolai

The oldest son of the Rostov family, Nikolai becomes an officer in the army. He fights in war, hoping to gain glory as a hero, but he soon accepts that he is but a cog in the great machine of humanity.

Other, less common characters in this family include: Vera, the eldest daughter, who marries Berg; Petya the youngest child, who is excited to join the army, but is killed in battle; Sonya a poor cousin who was taken in by the Rostovs; Boris, a friend of the Countess, who starts in the novel as a nobody and becomes a career military officer.

The Kuragin (*cure-AWG-in*) Family

Prince Vassily (vas-SILLY)

Hellene and Anatole's father, Vassily is an experienced courtier who works to make a good life for his children.

Anatole (ana-TOLL-eh)

Son of Vassily, Anatole is very handsome and he knows it. He tries to seduce Natasha.

Helene

A woman known for her great beauty, Helene marries Pierre, only to immediately start cheating on him. She dies of mysterious causes, officially from a heart attack.

Themes

Genius vs. Chaos

Tolstoy talks again and again about the real cause of victory or defeat. Some people are called geniuses, like Napoleon, who history calls a great military leader. But Tolstoy shows him to be a glory hungry man whose instructions often didn't make any sense. Napoleon stayed so far away during battle that his orders would be obsolete before even reaching the right people.

Instead, Tolstoy says, victory is often won through a chance culmination of many small events, most of which no one person can control. Kutuzov, a man criticized by historians, was, in Tolstoy's eyes, a great leader because he understood the chaotic nature of war. He took a more relaxed view of battle command.

Destiny vs. Free Will

Take the above theme and expand it out to more than just warfare, and you have a debate on destiny verses free will. What makes men and nations do what they do? What force moves peoples in one way or another? This is a big question Tolstoy highlights. Many time his characters feel overpowered by some great power or force, as if their path is out of their control.

Truth vs. History

Tolstoy constantly criticizes historians in this book, posing the question: how do we know what really happened in the past? Really, how can we be sure that what historians say is true at all? Historians remember the people and events that they want to highlight, ignoring all the other events and causes.

War vs. Humanity

The brutality of war in contrasted with moments of human connection. We see captures treating their prisoners with kindness. We see Russian soldiers feeding and caring for starving French soldiers. We listen in as French and Russian soldiers tell jokes to each other from their trenches.

Chapter Summaries

The chapter summaries below are grouped by book. There are fifteen books in War and Peace, each book having up to 25 chapters. Since the chapter numbering restarts with each book (meaning there are 15 chapter 1's), the book divisions really help you not to get lost.

Book I (1805)

In this first book, 25 chapters long, Tolstoy introduces the man characters of War and Peace through a series of parties and conversations. The first six chapters focus on a party thrown by Anna Pavlovna.

In **Chapter 1**, Anna Pavlovna welcomes the first guest, Prince Vassily. They talk about Napoleon and Vassily's kids, which are always causing him trouble. Anna suggests he marry his youngest son to the youngest Bolkonsky daughter. In **Chapter 2**, Prince Vassily's daughter, Helene, arrives, along with Liza Bolkonsky. Liza is pregnant, but still flirting with all the men at the party. The next guest is Pierre Bezukhov, the illegitimate son of a Count. He acts rudely and kind of makes scene, stressing Anna. He continues to act inappropriately in **Chapter 3**, because, as most of the groups listens to a Frenchman tell a story about Napoleon, Pierre gets into an argument with another guest. Anna has to break it up. Liza's husband, Prince Andrei Bolkonsky arrives. While Liza's flirting works with everyone else, Andrei pays no attention her. He only smiles when he meets his old friend, Pierre. They even make dinner plans. Vassily tells Anna that she must work with Pierre to make him more socially proper and less rude.

In **Chapter 4**, On his way out of the party, Prince Vassily is cornered by an old aristocrat woman, Princess Drubetskoy. He begs him to make her son Boris a guardsman. Because Vassily owes the Princess' family, he agrees. Meanwhile, the Frenchman and Anna criticize Napoleon before the group. Pierre steps up and defends Napoleon, calling him a great man. Prince Andrei sides with Pierre, probably because he doesn't like the Frenchman very much. Ippolit manages to change the topic by telling a silly joke. Ippolit ends up looking like an idiot, but his stupidity also seems like some kind of social genius.

Finally, in **Chapters 5 and 6**, the party ends and everyone starts to leave. While Prince Andrei continues to ignore his wife, Liza, Anna and Liza have talked about a possible marriage between Prince Vassily's son, Anatole and Liza'a sister-in-law. The guests leave in groups. It appears that Ippolit has some kind of romantic relationship with Liza behind Andrei's back. After the party, Andrei and Pierre are talking when Liza bursts in and starts up a fight with her husband. She is not happy that he plans on going to war. When the fight ends and Liza leaves, Andrei tells Pierre that he regrets getting married and that Pierre should never marry. He also advises Pierre to not spend time with Anatole, Vassily's son. Pierre leaves Andrei's place and goes straight to a big, drunken party at Anatole's. There, a drunk man is tied to a bear and thrown into a river.

The next several chapters focus on a double name-day party with the Rostov's in Moscow. The festivities introduce yet more characters, since few characters overlap between the two parties. But thing end with a death in the family.

In **Chapters 7 and 8**, Count Rostov greets each arriving guest in the same way, formally saying the same things to each person. Pierre is at this party, and his father, Count Bezukhov, is on his deathbed. Everyone's talking about Pierre'r rude behavior at Anna Pavlovna's party, as well as the prank with the bear at the party. Although Count Bezukhov has many illegitimate children, Pierre is his favorite, and so Pierre has a good chance of inheriting the count's title and riches.

Count Rostov teases his son Nikolai about joining the army, in **Chapter 9** though Nikolai says he won't go. Nikolai and his cousin, Sonya, are obviously in love, and Sonya gets upset when Julie Karagin flirts with him. When the Karagin's leave, Countess Rostov is happy about it, since they are very rude.

In **Chapter 10**, Natasha hides behind a plant, watching Sonya and Kikolai kiss. She calls Boris over and kisses him. He says that they can't kiss anymore, but when she is old, then plan to get married. Vera breaks up the kissing among the teenagers in **Chapter 11**, saying their too young for such things. Natasha argues with her sister. We also learn that poor Boris, who will now enter the army as an officer, doesn't have the money for equipment that he needs. His only hope is to get money from his godfather, the dying Count Bezukhov. In **Chapter 12**, Boris is dragged into the room to see Count Bezukhov. His mom is going to try to get the money Boris needs to go off to the military.

Boris and Pierre meet for the first time in **Chapter 13**, Pierre says that he doesn't want money, but he is upset that his father hasn't asked to see him, even though the Count is dying. Boris' mother hopes they'll inherit some money, but Boris doesn't know why they would. In **Chapter 14**, Countess Rostov gets the money Boris needs and gives it to Boris' mother. They cry together with joy.

In **Chapter 15**, everyone is waiting for dinner to begin. Pierre walks into the room and starts acting rude (like always), and an older woman named Marya Dmitrievna Akhhrosimov comes in an reproves Pierre for his stunt with the bear. Dinner begins in **Chapter 16**, and the conversation turns to the war. Nikolai says one of the most quoted lines from the book: "…the Russians must either die or conquer," a very pro-war statement. Little Natasha breaks the serious feel of the conversation when she asks her mother what's for dessert. Everyone laughs at her. After dinner, **Chapter 17** shows us a card game among the adults, while the children sing songs. Natasha finds Sonya is crying because she fears that Nikolai will end up marrying Julie. (Sonya and Nikolai are second cousins, so that makes things difficult.) After songs and games, the dancing begins.

Meanwhile, in **Chapter 18**, Count Bezukhov has his sixth stroke, leaving him right on death's door. His last rights begin. Prince Vassily, the closest legal relative to the dying Count, is interested about where the will is. He's worried that Pierre might inherit the title and riches. His fears are fueled by a rumor that the Count has sent a letter to the Emperor, asking to make Pierre legitimate, meaning Pierre might get everything. Vassily is talking wth Catiche, who also starts to freak out. In **Chapter 19**, Pierre and Princess Drubetskoy are on their way to Count Bezukhov's house, since he's finally called to see Pierre. Pierre sneaks into the house, going through servants' rooms to get to his father's room. Everyone is treating Pierre strangely, expecting that he will become a count before the night is out.

The climaxing moment comes in **Chapters 20 and 21**, as everyone prepares for the Count's passing. The final ceremony happens, and Pierre cries when he sees how his father is. Vassily and Catiche try and get the will before anyone else, in order to scam Pierre out of the money. But Princess Drubetskoy is on Pierre's side and stops their plan. In the end, the Count dies and Pierre is pronounced heir. In one night, he's gone from illegitimate son to rich count.

In the final chapters of Book I, we are taken to Bleak Hills along with Prince Andrei and the still pregnant Liza. They are visiting Andrei's family. His father, Prince Bolkonsky, was long ago banished from city life, so he now lives in this country estate. In **Chapter 22**, the Prince is talking to his daughter, Andrei's sister, Marya (the one that was suggested for Anatole to marry), teaching her math. She gets a letter from Julie Karagin, who tells all about the name-day party in Moscow and Pierre's surprise inheritance. Julie hopes she'll marry Pierre, and she tells of the arrangements being made for Marya to marry Anatole. Marya write back, saying that if God wishes her to marry, she'll do her best.

Andrei and Liza arrive in **Chapter 23**, they find Marya, who cries when she sees Liza, showing just how lonely she is. Andrei goes to find his father and starts bragging to him about the military strategies the Russians will use against the French. The father is unimpressed. Everyone gets together when dinner is served in **Chapter 24**. Andrei makes fun of his father before the old man arrives to the table. Prince Bolkonsky talks to Liza, but when she starts talking about city gossip, he changes the subject. He wants to talk about war. He was a general in the old days and, now that his son, Andrei, is going off to war tomorrow, he complains about modern war tactics and modern soldiers.

In **Chapter 25**, Andrei is packing to go off to war. Marya tells him that he should be more respectful of their father and more loving to his wife. She also gives him a necklace with Christ on it. Andrei is not at all religious, the exact opposite of Marya, but he takes the icon from his sister and promises to wear it. So Andrei goes off to war, leaving his poor wife in the country, away from the city social life she loves. He kisses Liza and she faints.

Book II

The Russian army arrives in Austria in **Chapter 1**. They just finished marching 20 miles without sleep, only to receive word that they are to be inspected right away. There is some confusion as to whether the soldiers should be inspected in the clothes they've just marched in or in their dress uniforms. In **Chapter 2**, Kutuzov, the leader, Andrei and the Austrian general inspect the men. It is clear that the men like Kutuzov. They notice that the men need new boots, since they've marched a long way and have no replacement footwear. Marching music begins and the men march on. In **Chapter 3**, we see that there is a lot of friction between Kutuzov and the Austrian general. They constantly fight with words, but everything covered by fake politeness. Finally, Kutuzov sends Andrei to write up a memo; Andrei and Kutuzov are on very good terms because Kutuzov once fought alongside Andrei's father. Suddenly, General Mack (an ally) arrives, having survived a great defeat at the hands of Napoleon.

In **Chapter 4**, we jump from Andrei in Austria to Nikolai in Poland. He has a friend with him, named Vaska Denisov, who stays in the same house with him. Although they hear about General Mack's defeat to Napoleon, it doesn't affect them directly like it does to Andrei. Vaska comes home from gambling, having lost a lot of money. He puts his wallet under his pillow. A man named Lieutenant Telyanin visits and shows Nikolai how to shoe a horse. Later, when Vaska has to pay his gambling debts, he realizes his wallet is gone; they immediately suspect Telyanin. He tracks Telyanin down to a local bar, but Telyanin makes himself look so pitiful that Vaska lets him keep the money. Because of the big scandal Nikolai makes about the theft, he is ordered by his commander to deny the whole thing in **Chapter 5**, after all, the theft story threatens the reputation of the whole regiment. Nikolai is put in a position in which he must choose between his own honor and that of the group. The problem is interrupted when they all receive orders to march to Austria right away. The men are all excited to finally see some action.

In **Chapter 6**, we go back to General Kutuzov's army, marching toward Vienna. Every bridge they cross, they burn after. They get close to the town of Enns, and as the officers look over their troops, they can see the French camps on the next hill over. They are crossing one last bridge, and the enemy starts to fire on them, but they are still too far away to hit the Russians. Nesvitsky tries to cross the bridge in **Chapter 7**, but the soldiers cross slowly. When an enemy round hits the water nearby, everyone starts to panic. Vaska Denisov (from Polond with Nikolai) comes to help get people across, and Nesvitsky gets to deliver orders to men on the other side of the river. In **Chapter 8**, Nikolai is in the last group to cross the bridge, the French hot on their tails. The French are firing, but they're still just too far away to hit anyone. Finally, Nikolai realizes that no one has burned the bridge, like they were supposed to. He goes back with some volunteers to set fire to the bridge, cutting off the French behind them, but now they are in range. Bombs and shrapnel fall all around them, and Nikolai starts to panic. Some men die, but the bridge ends up on fire--mission accomplished, and with limited casualties.

In **Chapter 9**, we see that the Russians are in full retreat from the French. As they run away, the French catch up and there's a battle between the front forces of the French and the rear guard of the Russians. Kutuzov fights as little as possible to increase the distance between his men and the French. They finally arrive on the banks of the Danube. They cross, leaving the French on the other side. Only a small force, under and French man named Mortier, is on the same side with the Russians. Kuturov attacks Mortier, gaining victory, a victory that ups morale for the Russian men. Because he performed well in this battle against Mortier, Andrei is rewarded with an assignment: go to the Austrian Emperor and report on the victory. He goes to Brunn and reports the victory, but no one is impressed. Instead, Andrei sees all the politics behind the war.

Andrei's disappointment gets worse in **Chapter 10**, in which he stays with a diplomat named Bilibin. Bilibin explains why none of the Austrian leaders care about the victory against Mortier. First, they don't like Russian victories, because the Austrians want all the credit. Second, Vienna (the capital of Austria) is under French control, and Bilibin says Napoleon is soon to win the war. So the Austrians don't care about a minor Russian victory. As can be expected, Andrei is depressed after hearing this.

In **Chapter 11**, Andrei is preparing to talk to the Austrian Emperor himself. He chats with Bilibin and some other diplomats, including a character we've seen before: Ippolit. Ippolit was trying to seduce Andrei's wife in the early chapters, and Andrei seems upset (understandably) about this. But he also sees Ippolit as a kind of joker, not to be taken seriously. Andrei goes to see the Emperor, and they meet in **Chapter 12**. The Emperor doesn't care at all about Andrei's report, but after the meeting, other diplomats pay much more attention to Andrei. When he gets back to Bilibin's house, he finds that everyone is packing up to leave, since Napoleon has managed to cross the river from Vienna and is coming their way. Andrei can't believe the Napoleon managed to cross that bridge, since is was heavily guarded and wired with explosives. But cross it he has. Andrei wants to leave, imagining he can become a hero by joining the army and fighting off the French.

Andrei rides back to find the Russian army in **Chapter 13**. He happens upon a situation in which a Russian officer is drunk and beating a man up, and Andrei manages to stop him. Later, he shares a meal with Nesvitsky, a man we met in an earlier chapter, but briefly. After, Andrei goes and finds Kuturov, who invites him to ride in his carriage with him. They talk, and Kuturov wants to know about Andrei's meet with the Emperor.

Chapter 14 gives us an overview of the next leg of the war. Kuturov is in a difficult position. The French are in hot pursuit, and the Russians are about to be surrounded. As they flee Austria, their only hope is to send a small force to stall the French forces, allowing time for Kuturov and the rest of the army to get to the next town and prepare to defend it. He sends Bagration with four thousand men to stall the French, being lead by Murat. Murat makes a three-day truce with Bagration, which the Russians really need. Kuturov sends word to "pretend" to surrender to the French to buy time and launch a surprise attack. Murat falls for it, but Napoleon sends word that this is a trick. The chapter ends with the threat of battle in the air.

We zero in on Andrei again in **Chapter 15**. We find out he's gone with Bagration to meet Murat in battle. Andrei chooses to lead and fight on the front lines, and he rides out to scout out the land and place troops. He gets all the way to the front lines and sees something amazing. The Russians and French are so close to each other that they are actually talking to each other! Guns and cannons are pointed at each other, of course, but the men are actually joking and teasing each other. Andrei goes back to a position where he can see the entire battlefield in **Chapter 16**. He makes some notes on troop positions, along with some suggestions. He overhears some officers in a nearby tent talking about the afterlife. Just then, a French cannonball hits the ground close to the tent, sending the men running out in panic.

The battle begins in **Chapter 17**. The French are beginning the attack, and Andrei rides out with Bagration and some other officers to the front lines. A cannonball kills a man on a horse, but the rest continue, unfazed. Bagration shows courage and great leadership skills during the battle. Though they are outnumbered and losing the battle, he is calmly giving orders. The morale stays high because of him, and Andrei really starts to respect the man. In **Chapter 18**, Bagration sends a few regiments to fight, allowing others to retreat. He also shows he's not afraid to give orders from the front lines, where the danger is extremely high. The Russians get a break in Chapter 19, because they set fire to a nearby town. The French are distracted by trying to put out the fire, meaning the Russians can retreat. On the opposite side of the battle, however, the French are advancing and killing many Russians. Bagration sends messages to that side, but the messenger never makes it over there. Meanwhile, two men fight over who should be in charge of that area of the battle. Because of their fighting, the French surround them.

In that surrounded group is young Nikolai Rostov. He is injured right away, and he's almost killed by French soldiers. He manages to run away and hide in some bushes, where other Russian soldiers hide, as well.

In **Chapter 20**, we see the bravery of several men. First, there's Nikolai. When the Russians are completely surrounded by French men, and outnumbered, Nikolai leads the Russian soldiers that were in the bushes with such passion and energy that the French actually retreat. Another brave man here is Dolokhov, a man that was involved in the "bear" incident at the beginning of the book (in Anatole's party, in Petersburg). As a result, he was demoted. Now, he fights with amazing courage, killing some French soldiers and taking a French officer hostage. Finally, there's Captain Tushin, one of the men that were in the tent that was almost hit by a cannonball a couple of chapters back. He commands a group of cannons, right in the middle of the battle, hammering away at the French. Andrei rides in and tells Tushin that he was supposed to retreat a while ago, but the messenger never got to them. Andrei and Tushin stay there in the battle until all the cannons are removed. The battle, seen through Andrei's eyes, is horrific, littered with body parts and blood and smoke.

Bagration's men have done their job, stalling the French, but at great cost. In **Chapter 21**, they are marching away from battle. Nikolai gets a ride on a wagon. His arm is badly hurt, though he says it's only bruised. Tushin is called into Bagration's tent, at which point Bagration yells at Tushin because he didn't retreat when ordered to. The messenger that never delivered his message is there, but he's lying about what happened. Although we know Tushin was a hero in battle, he doesn't defend himself now because he doesn't want to get another officer (the coward messenger) in trouble. Andrei defends Tushin, though. After the meeting, Andrei walks off, disappointed, since the "glory" of war isn't what he'd imagined. Meanwhile, Nikolai is still badly hurt, to the point that he's hallucinating.

Book III

Book III sends us back to the "peace" part of War and Peace, but showing us what's happening with Pierre, who, in **Chapter 1**, is being kept on a tight leach by Prince Vassily. Vassily is managing all of Pierre's newly inherited accounts and responsibilities, pocketing some of the money along the way. Vassily is also trying to arrange a marriage between Helene, his beautiful daughter, and Pierre. So everywhere Pierre goes, Helene is sent with him. Although Pierre thinks she is not very smart (and perhaps having an incest-like relationship with her brother, Anatole), he also realizes that he finds her very attractive. He worries that he's already somehow committed to marrying her, a thought that both scares and excites him. Things move very fast in **Chapter 2**, in which Vassily manipulates Pierre into marrying Helene. Pierre is still unsure, but he likes her more and more. Finally, after Helene's name-day party, he kind of goes with the flow, agreeing to marry her. The chapter ends showing the couple married and living together, just one month later.

In Chapter 3, Vassily moves on to trying to get his son, Anatole married. We remember that Anatole is supposed to marry Marya, Andrei's sister, who is very plain looking. Prince Bolkonsky (Andrei's father) doesn't like Vassily at all. When they do arrive in Bolkonsky's estate, Anatole keeps asking about Marya's appearance. Meanwhile, Liza and Bourienne help Marya dress in a way that makes her more attractive. They eventually give up, meaning Marya is hopeless. Marya is very excited about getting married. She imagines herself having children, but immediately feels shame for what she considers dirty thoughts. Marya and Anatole meet in **Chapter 4**. Liza, Bourienne, Bolkonsky, and Vassily are there, too. The two fathers agree that their children can marry if they want to. Meanwhile, Bourienne is trying to seduce Anatole for herself, which seems to be working.

The next morning, in **Chapter 5**, Anatole and Bourienne go off alone together. Marya talks to her father, who isn't sure she should marry Anatole (unless she really wants to). When she finds Anatole and Bourienne kissing, she decides not to ever get married. She'll sacrifice herself and stay with her father forever. She also announces that she supports Anatole and Bourienne getting married, if they want.

We move on the Rostovs in **Chapter 6**. They receive a letter from Nikolai about how he was injured (but healed now) and how he's now been promoted of officer. The family is very happy about this. They send supplies and money to Nikolai via Boris. Boris gets to package to Nikolai's army (in Olmutz) in **Chapter 7**. He talks with Berg and Nikolai. Nikolai tells about how he was injured, a story that he can't help but embellish. Andrei come into the conversation and calls Nikolai on his tall tale. Nikolai gets very angry after Andrei leaves, but he also respects him.

The Austrian and Russian emperors inspect the army in **Chapter 8**. Nikolai is there, and he feels such devotion for his Tsar that he thinks he could die if the man would just look at him.

While with Andrei in **Chapter 9**, Boris tries to get a better position in the military. He sees first hand that the official rank of a man (like General) isn't as important as the connections a man has. So even Generals listen to Andrei. Boris is very excited about being this close to power. In **Chapter 10**, Nikolai also gets close to power when he is inspected by the emperor, and he loves his leader so much that be begins fantasizing about dying in front of the Emperor or saving his life somehow.

In **Chapter 11**, the emperor gets sick from seeing all the dead from battle. Napoleon sends an envoy of peace, but the peace talks fall through. So the army marches on. Kuturov thinks the army should wait. But others think they should attack now, believing Napoleon's attamps at peace mean he's weak. The decision is made to attack, but Kuturov predicts that the battle will be lost for the Russians. The battle plans are made in **Chapter 12**. No one listens to Kuturov, so he falls asleep in the meeting. Andrei can't get a word in either. He is upset because all the generals are thinking more about their own political plans instead of the smartest battle strategy. Even though he knows he may die the next day (the day of the battle), Andrei hopes he can somehow save the day and become a military hero.

We jump back to Nikolai in **Chapter 13**. He's riding out to battle in the middle of the night, falling asleep on his horse. When shouts and gunfire are heard from the French side, they hurry out to find out what's happening. The French are also lighting fires, and no one knows why. Nikolai volunteers to go and see if the sharpshooters are still where they were or if the French are retreating. He rides out and is shot at, forced to return. The truth is, Napoleon himself is riding out to visit the troops on the French side, and the men are firing weapons and lighting fires in their excitement. It's also revealed that Napoleon has a plan to defeat the Russians. The next morning, in **Chapter 14**, the Russians march out to fight the French, but a thick fog makes them unable to see. They think the French are still far off when they are really right in front of them. They can't prepare to fight because they're surprised. Meanwhile Napoleon sees everything from a nearby hill. He waits until the Russians are close, and then he gives the order to attack.

In **Chapter 15**, Kutuzov is ordering his men to form up, because he thinks the French are closer than everyone says. The emperors ride up and order him to move him men forward. He does so. Andrei is there, expecting to be a hero today. In **Chapter 16**, the French attack! Thing get bad fast for the Russians. Kutuzov is hurt, and Andrei notices that many Russians are already retreating. He picks up a fallen flag and orders the men forward and the listen to him. Andrei's being a hero, until he's hit in the head and falls down. He sees the infinite sky, a moment of religious clarity, and passes out.

In **Chapter 17**, Nikolai is sent to deliver a message to Kutuzov or the Emperor. He seems to get lost in the fog. He sees Austrians and Russians shooting each other. He finally heads toward the hill where Kutuzov is supposed to be, even though there are French cannons up there. In **Chapter 18**, Nikolai continues to search for either Kutuzov or the Emperor, but everyone is lost and confused. He finally sees the Emperor, but he's too shy to walk over and talk to him. Meanwhile, the battle is lost. Some men are trapped on a bridge over a frozen river. Because they're being killed by French cannons and guns, they jump down onto the ice, which breaks. All the men are either shot or drown.

In **Chapter 19**, Andrei wakes up and is surrounded by French. He's visited by Napoleon himself-- Andrei's personal hero. Napoleon has Andrei taken care of. Andrei doesn't care about all that. He's 'seen death' in the sky, and even the great Napoleon is small in comparison.

Book IV

It's 1806, and Nikolai is returning home from war in
Chapter 1. Everyone comes out of the house to
welcome him when he rides up on his horse. He's
brought a friend home with him--Denisov. The next
morning, Sonya and Natasha are excited to wake the
boys up. Sonya and Nikolai mutually agree to not be
engaged anymore, although they still like each other.
Natasha, who used to like Boris, is now having a
crush on Denisov. In **Chapter 2**, we see how Nikolai
is living a good life in Moscow, the life of a single,
rich, attractive, young man. Nikolai's father, count
Rostov, is planning a party dinner for General
Bagration at an exclusive club. Nikolai visits him.
Everyone is praising Bagration for his victory in the
war (remember, the defeat that was really a victory
because it held off the French army long enough for
the Russian forces to retreat to safety). Everyone is
talking about Andrei's death at such a young age.
(Although no one really knows he is really dead at all,
everyone assumes it.) The party starts in **Chapter 3**.
Pierre (whose wife is apparently cheating on him)
feels uncomfortable in such a dinner, since everyone
is much older than himself. Bagration arrives and
everyone toasts to him again and again until they are
all drunk. Count Rostov starts crying when he
proposes a toast to the Russian Emperor.

At the close of the dinner, in **Chapter 4**, Pierre is seated close to Dolokhov, the man that is supposedly having and affair with Pierre's wife. Pierre is getting angrier and angrier at him, and Dolokhov is really rubbing it in. He even toasts to beautiful women and their lovers at the table. Eventually, Pierre--so sure Dolokhov is guilty of sleeping with his wife-- challenges him to a duel the next day. Pierre can't sleep that night, knowing the duel is the next day. The Duel happens in **Chapter 5**. Pierre shoots Dolokhov in the side, while Dolokhov misses Pierre completely. Dolokhov actually cries in the carriage ride away from the duel, not wanting to die.

Pierre realizes that his life is not going the way he wanted it to go in **Chapter 6**. He is in a loveless marriage with a woman he considers gross and rude. He decides he's going to leave her. When Helene comes to see him, she is angry about the duel. He gets so angry that he tries to kill her; she runs away before he can do so. He leaves for Petersburg, leaving Helene more than half his fortune.

In **Chapter 7**, we jump back to Bleak Hills, where Liza will have her baby any day now. Andrei is still thought dead, and everyone reacts to this assumption differently. No one wants to tell Liza that her husband is probably dead, even though Bolkonsky orders a grave for him. Liza goes into labor in **Chapter 8**. They call a doctor from Moscow, since Liza insists on not using a midwife. She screams in pain the whole night, and Marya prays for her sister-in-law in her room. The next morning, someone arrives. Marya thinks it's only the doctor, but it turns out that Andrei is in the same carriage! Liza has the baby in **Chapter 9**, at the cost of her own life. Andrei is both happy to have a child, but regretful about the way he treated his wife. Liza is buried and the baby is baptized when a week old.

In **Chapter 10**, the young men prepare to go to war again. Throughout the winter, Napoleon has been getting closer to Russia. Meanwhile, Nikolai's father is able save him from punishment for his involvement in the Pierre-Dolokhov duel, since duels were outlawed at that time. Love is in the air in **Chapter 11**. Dolokhov propses to Sonya. When Nikolai hears about this, he is at first upset, but he later realizes that, if he won't marry her after all, this is a good marriage for Sonya. But the point is moot when Sonya rejects Dolokhov. Nikolai and Sonya talk. She says she loves him, as he does her, but neither really wants to marry the other. At a dance in **Chapter 12**, Denisov and Natasha spend all the time dancing together.

In **Chapter 13**, Dolokhov invites Nikolai to a party, in which everyone is gambling. What Nikolai doesn't know is this is a plan of Dolokhov to get revenge for Sonya's rejecting him. He's going to gamble a wealth of money away from Nikolai. Nikolai suspects that Dolokhov cheats somehow, but he sits down to play cards with him. Nikolai quickly gets 1,600 rubles in the hole, which is bad because he only has 1,200 rubles. In **Chapter 14**, Nikolai ends up 43,000 rubles in dept, and Dolokhov lets it slip that this is really all about Sonya. Nikolai promises to bring the money the next day.

Nikolai is not happy when he gets home in **Chapter 15**. The rest are singing and listening to music. Nikolai forgets about his problems for a moment as he sings along. Nikolai's father gets home in **Chapter 16**, and when Nikolai tells him how much money he needs to pay off his debt, his father starts to get very worried. Nikolai starts sobbing. Meanwhile, Natasha is excited because Denisov has proposed to her. But her mom talks her out of it, saying she's too young for marriage (15). So Natasha turns Denisov down. He leaves for the army the next day, and Nikolai leaves too, as soon as his father can get the dept money together and send it off to Dolokhov.

BOOK V

It's now the end of 1806 to the beginning of 1807, and the characters of this novel continue to change and develop in very unexpected ways. Take, for example, what happens to Pierre. In **Chapter 1**, after Pierre's fight with Helene, he goes to Petersburg. He has to stop at an inn for a change of horses. While he's waiting, he's very deep in thought (as he should be, since his life has changed a lot lately). A man comes and sits close to him, reading. In **Chapter 2**, this older man strikes up a conversation with Pierre, admitting that he knows not only who Pierre is, but also what he has done (the riches, the duel, and the fight with his newly-married wife). The man doesn't explain how he knows these things. He does talk about belief in good and evil, as well as belief in God. The man ends up convincing Pierre to join the freemasons. This old man turns out to be a very famous Mason himself--Bazdeev.

In **Chapters 3 and 4**, Pierre is given man books and papers on the Mason to read and think about, and then he is finally initiated into the organization. He's blindfolded and taken to a secret place, where he is lectured on the meaning of the Masons. When the blindfold is taken off, Pierre is officially a Freemason.

In **Chapter 5**, Pierre is visited by Prince Vassily, who tries to convince him to fix his relationship with his wife. Pierre basically kicks him out of the house. He then starts giving his money to others.

Meanwhile, news has spread about Pierre's duel, and he's being made out to be the bad guy. In **Chapter 6**, at another of Anna Pavlovna's parties, Boris (who has been climbing the ranks in the military) puts on a good show with songs and stories, and he catches the attention of Helene, who asks him to dinner the next evening. Still at the party, Helene again asks Boris to dinner in **Chapter 7**. Boris goes the next evening, and is kind of ignored by Helene most of the time. But she asks him to come back the next week, and he agrees.

Now that Russia is forced to defend their own boarder from the French, Prince Bolkonsky is out as head of the militia in his area. In **Chapter 8**, Andrei and Marya struggle to nurse baby Nikolai out of a bad fever. Even when he gets a letter from his father, telling him to deliver a message, he refuses because of his baby. In **Chapter 9**, Andrei reads a letter from Bilibin, which is long and full of criticisms about the way the military works. When Andrei goes back to check on his son, he finds out that the baby is getting better; the fever has broken.

In **Chapter 10**, Pierre visits some of his land, which is run by stewards, and announces that he wants to make some compassionate reforms for the serfs (the farmers that work the land, just a little better than slaves). The stewards, though, just steal from Pierre and make no changes. When Pierre visits, the stewards put on a big show to make him happy. Happy with himself, Pierre goes to visit his old friend Andrei in **Chapter 11**. Andrei is bitter about life and war. They have a big philosophical discussion about good and evil. They take a carriage ride in **Chapter 12**, heading to Andrei's father's estate, which is nearby. That's also where Andrei's baby is. In the carriage, Pierre talks to Andrei about the Masons, and Andrei seems interested. In **Chapter 13**, Pierre and Andrei get to Bolkonsky's estate, where Marya is being visited by some people of God. Pierre and Andrei make fun of them until they get ready to leave, at which point Pierre apologizes about being rude. Prince Bolkonsky arrives in **Chapter 14**, and they all have a happy dinner together. Pierre feels good with them there, in Bleak Hills.

In **Chapter 15**, we see Nikolai returning to his regiment, which he is very happy to see again. Spirits are high in the camp, although there is very little food; half of the soldiers are lost to starvation and disease. Nikolai finds a family nearby. The old man of the family is sick, so Nikolai takes the man, his daughter, and the daughter's baby to his hut to get better. Nikolai even protects the daughter from fellow soldiers. Because of the hard conditions, the men live in trenches. In **Chapter 16**, Denisov rides off with some of his men and hijacks a provisions transport to give his regiment something to eat. The higher-ups don't think this is very heroic, though, saying this is grounds for court martial. Denisov gets a minor wound in the next fight, and he uses that as an excuse to stay in the infirmary.

Some months pass, and Russia is losing the war. Nikolai rides out to see Denisov in **Chapter 17**. The infirmary tent is disgusting, smelling of rotten flesh and death. Nikolai is finally taken to see Denisov in **Chapter 18**, and Denisov is a changed man. He has become obsessed with his court case, and he gives a petition for clemency to Nikolai to give to the emperor. Nikolai goes to the city of Tilsit with the letter in **Chapter 19**, where both Emperor Alexander and Napoleon are for a treaty signing. Nikolai tries to just give the letter to Boris, but he feels uncomfortable around the man. (After Boris' ordeal with Nikolai's sister, who can blame him?) In **Chapter 20**, Nikolai decides to hand the letter directly to the Emperor. After some hassle in the house the Emperor is staying, Nikolai finally gets to see him, only to hear that Alexander will not grant a pardon. Despite the rejection to his friend, Denisov, Nikolai runs after Alexander in the streets, overjoyed to be with his leader.

In **Chapter 21**, Nikolai witnesses the meeting between Alexander and Napoleon. Nikolai doesn't like Napoleon at all, not the way he talks to Alexander (like they are equals). Nikolai is not happy about the whole think, especially when some random soldier is chosen by Napoleon to be the "bravest Russian soldier." He begins to remember the hospital he visited to find Denisov, and he wonders if all the death is for nothing.

BOOK VI

About a year has passed, and Russia and France are still allies, helping each other. There is even talk of a marriage alliance between Alexander's family and Napoleon. Meanwhile, in **Chapter 1**, Andrei is making reforms, the same changes Pierre wanted to make but couldn't. Andrei sees a tree one day while riding along the road. It's old and withered, and he thinks of himself as the same, even though he's only 31. In **Chapter 2**, Andrei visits Count Rostov, and he's very distracted by how joyful Natasha is. He stays the night in the house, unable to deal with his emotions. Andrei leaves early the next day, in **Chapter 3**. On his way home, he sees the old tree from before, but now it's full of green leaves. He decides he should continue living, as well, and he gets very frustrated with his life.

In **Chapter 4**, Andrei travels to Petersburg. He has some ideas about how to reform the military. He tries to take these ideas to the Emperor, but he's turned down. He goes then to the minister of war, but, there, his ideas are also turned down. But Andrei is appointed to the committee on military regulations. In **Chapter 5**, since Andrei is now living in Petersburg, he meets a powerful man named Speransky. Speransky thinks the reforms in the government are good (like leaders must pass a test to prove competence, instead of just being born in the right family). Andrei doesn't fully agree, but he likes Speransky so much, he goes along with the idea. Andrei is known as a modern reformer now, anyway, because of the changes he's been making on his estates.

Because of his friendship with Speransky, in **Chapter 6,** Andrei is appointed to be head of the legislative commission, meaning he gets to help write the laws of the country.

In **Chapter 7**, we switch to Pierre, who, because of his zeal for Mason teachings, has become the head of the Petersburg Masons. He's trying to put his life back on the right spiritual path, so he travels abroad for a year to learn the ways of Masons elsewhere. When he gets back, he tells others in the lodge about changes he wants to make. But no one is really interested in what he has to say, since most people just joined the Masons to make connections and get prominence. Pierre leaves the lodge after his ideas are rejected. Depressed from this meeting, Pierre doesn't leave his house for three days in **Chapter 8**. After receiving various messages from his wife, Helene, Pierre decides to reconcile with her. They end up together again, but they're not sleeping together still, since Pierre feels he must be free from all lust.

In **Chapter 9**, we see that Helene quickly becomes a social queen in Petersburg. She throws many parties, and everyone wants to be around her, something Pierre doesn't understand because he sees her as of little intelligence. Also, Boris comes often to the house, which frustrates Pierre. In **Chapter 10,** Pierre has dreams that lead him revelations. He interprets that he must not be attached to material things, and he also decides he must start sleeping with his wife again, as part of the husband's duty.

In **Chapter 11**, the Rostovs move to Petersburg for a time. Berg and Vera are to get married, and the family is happy for them, although they are still very poor because of having to pay Nikolai's enormous debt. Boris notices Natasha again in **Chapter 12**. At the beginning of the book, Boris was in love with her. Now, he's taken a new interest in this older, more mature young woman, and he visits the family's house every day. Natasha's mom sets her straight in **Chapter 13**, explaining that Boris is a bad match for her and that Boris needs to stop coming over so often. Natasha comes to understand and agree with he mother. In **Chapters 14 and 15,** Natasha gets to go to her first major social event: a ball on New Year's Eve, in 1810. Natasha sees Pierre and his wife Helene, Helene's brother, Anatole, as well as Andrei. She is overwhelmed by the party. When the Emperor arrives, in **Chapters 16 and 17**, the dancing starts. Pierre get's Andrei to ask Natasha to dance. After that, Natasha dances with all kinds of men and boys. Andrei dances with her again before dinner is served, and he seems to be falling for her.

The next day, in **Chapter 18**, Andrei is having a major change in perspective. He isn't mystified by everything his old mentor, Speransky, anymore. He starts asking himself deep questions about the purpose of all his work in government reforms. Will that really make him happy? In **Chapter 19,** Andrei ends up visiting the Rostovs, and he feels very good there because of how the family is. He's also feeling something for Natasha. When Natasha sings a song for him after dinner, he's brought to tears. Andrei can't sleep that night, just thinking about how in love he is with that girl.

Meanwhile, in **Chapter 20,** Berg invites Pierre to dinner, and even though Helene already said no, Pierre accepts and goes. Remember Berg and Vera just got married, and this is their first social event. They're working very hard to make this feel like a good party, although it all feels overdone and stilted. In **Chapter 21,** Pierre is forced to play cards with an old general. Natasha is at this party, and Pierre sees that she's looking very blue…until Andrei walks up and says something to her. She perks up and looks happy and beautiful again.

The next day, Andrei goes to the Rostovs and spends the day with them. In **Chapter 22**, it's obvious that he and Natasha are in love. She talks to her mom, and she's both in love and scared. Andrei goes and visits Pierre, telling him how he feels about Natasha. Pierre is happy for his friend, but he also feels bad for himself, since his life with Helene isn't all that good.

Andrei travels to see his father in **Chapter 23**. He asks his father permission to marry Natasha. His father says that's great, but he needs to wait a year to make sure the love is real. Andrei agrees, stays with his father, sister, and son for three weeks, and then he heads out to Natasha's house to propose. Natasha is very excited when her mother says yes. She even agrees to wait the year before the wedding.

In **Chapter 24**, Andrei decides not to announce the engagement for a while, so if things don't work out, Natasha's reputation won't be hurt. He leaves for Germany, and Natasha is greatly affected by his absence.

In **Chapter 25,** we see that Andrei's father, Prince Bolkonsky, is growing more and more bitter. The events of the recent war have really affected him, especially how Napoleon treated Emperor Alexander. Marya endure being with her father, relying on her spiritual faith. Some time later, in **Chapter 26**, Andrei sends a letter, telling her about his engagement with Natasha. Six months have passed, and he's still in love. He wants to get married sooner than the originally proposed year, but his father is being rude about the suggestion. He begins to taunt Marya, saying he's going to marry the servant lady of the house. Marya feels very depressed about all this. She even toys with the idea of leaving as a religious traveler. In the end, she decides she must stay with her father and baby nephew, though.

Book VII

We move from 1810 to 1811 in this seventh book. In **Chapter 1**, Nikolai's mom keeps begging him to come home and help manage the estate financially. His father is getting old and confused, and things are getting bad for them. He sees Sonya and Natasha, the former still pretty and in love with him, the latter happy and in love, waiting to marry Andrei. In **Chapter 2,** Nikolai makes a mess of trying to help the accounts. He throws the accountant out of the house, only to have to accept him back later.

Instead, Nikolai decides to go hunting. In **Chapter 3**, Nikolai starts to plan the hunt with, and Petya (who is now 13) and Natasha insist on going. In **Chapters 4 and 5**, Count Rostov gets ready to go, as well. They head out to hunt down some nearby wolves. They meet up with some relatives and join forces, the hunting party now becoming very large. They send their dogs into this patch of forest to kill or tire the wolves. The group of dogs splits up, making more confusion. A wolf runs out close to Count Rostov, who was not ready for such a close encounter. When the count lets the wolf go, Danilo, a servant of the Rostovs, reproves the Count. Later, when Nikolai's dogs corner the wolf, they tie it up to have it stuffed at home. Danilo apologizes to the Count.

In **Chapters 6 and 7**, the hunt continues, although Count Rostov himself has decided to go home. Nikolai runs into a neighbor that is not on good terms with the Rostov family. They decide to hunt together, trying to keep up polite appearances, even though the families are suing each other. When a hare is spotted, they have the dogs race. The winning dog (the one that caught the hare) belongs to Nikolai's relative, affectionately called "Uncle." The hunting over, the group stays at Uncle's house for dinner and some folk music. Nikolai is amazed when Natasha starts dancing to the Russian folk music, which really is amazing since the Russian aristocracy in those days was very sophisticated and frenchified. Nikolai and Natasha are called home by Mom and Dad. They take a carriage back to their estate, both very happy together.

In **Chapter 8,** Nikolai's mother tries to get him to agree to marry Julie Karagin, seeing this as a way to solve the families financial problems (since the Karagin's are rich). But Nikolai doesn't want that at all. He want's to be with Sonya. Meanwhile, Andrei writes Natasha to say that he has to stay abroad longer. In **Chapter 9,** Natasha is sad and lonely all through Christmas time. She wants Andrei back with her.

After Christmas, in **Chapter 10,** Natash, Sonya, and Nikolai talk about pleasant memories from their childhood. Their discussion is interrupted with the mummers arrive (people that dress up after Christmas time and sing songs for their neighbors. The three decide to go and join in the fun, making costumes for themselves. Nikolai starts falling more and more in love with Sonya. In **Chapter 11,** the group goes to another house nearby, there, the children tell them a ghost story about how the bathhouse is supposed to be haunted. Sonya volunteers to go investigate. Nikolai sneaks to the bathhouse first. When they meet, secretly, they kiss before returning to the others separately. Nikolai is sure he's completely in love with her now. They ride back home in **Chapter 12**. Natasha and Sonya talk about how they imagine their lives married in the future.

Not long after, in **Chapter 13**, Nikolai informs his mother that he'll marry Sonya or no one else. She is not happy about this, since Sonya has no money. She and Nikolai fight over Sonya, and Natasha is barely able to calm them down.

BOOK VIII

We're moving through 1811 to 1812. In **Chapter 1**, we see how Pierre has gotten very depressed about his own life after Andrei and Natasha got engaged. He goes back to Moscow, where he can be a little happier, partially to get away from his wife, who is always with other men. In **Chapter 2**, Prince Bolkonsky also moves into Moscow with Marya and the rest of the household. The prince continues to torture Marya, which he especially does by showing romantic advances toward Mlle. Bourienne. In **Chapter 3,** Prince Bolkonsky is growing more and more senile and paranoid. On his name day, he kicks out a doctor, claiming he is a spy. Everyone else just kind of rolls with it, trying to be understanding.

In the party, in **Chapter 4**, Marya is very depressed about her dad. When Pierre comes up and tries to start conversation, she breaks down and cries. In **Chapter 5,** Boris proposes to Julie Karagin. He's been desperate to marry a rich girl, and although Julie is ugly, he is willing to sacrifice for the riches. When he starts to hesitate, Julie gets him to pop the question by making him feel jealous, pretending to be with someone else. He proposes, and wedding plans get under way.

The Rostov's move to Moscow in **Chapter 6**, staying with Marya Dmitrievna Akhrosimov, an old friend of the family. Natasha and Sonya get some new dresses made. Natasha plans to go and visit her future in-laws, Andrei's family. When she does make that visit in **Chapter 7,** things don't go too well. Marya and Natasha dislike each other right away, and Prince Bolkonsky is only seen once for a momen, confused and wearing a bathrobe.

That same night, in **Chapter 8,** the girls go to the opera. Natasha and Sonya get everyone's attention with their youthful beauty. Natasha sees some familiar faces (to us; not necessarily to her), like Helene, Anatole, Boris and Julie. In **Chapter 9,** the first part of the opera must be a little boring to Natasha, since she's describing everything very dryly. When she sees Anatole (who seems to be interested in her), things change for her. In **Chapter 10,** Natasha is invited up to Helene's private box during the intermission, and She gets' a chance to meet Anatole. They are both very attracted to each other. Later, Natasha feels guilty when she remembers that she's still engaged to Andrei. We learn more about Anatole in **Chapter 11**. He was married before, but he left his wife and is living like a bachelor again. He wants to seduce Natasha, and he begins planning how he's going to get her into his bed.

In **Chapter 12,** the next day, Natasha is confused and excited about the night before. She wishes Andrei would come home from abroad. Helene comes over, and Natasha is excited to see her. Natasha goes to a party of Anatole's in **Chapter 13**. She's getting compliments from everyone about how pretty she is. Anatole asks her to dance, and he tells her he loves her. Later, he kisses her.

In **Chapter 14**, Natasha is very confused. She thinks she's now in love with Anatole. When she gets a love letter from her, she starts to forget all about Andrei. In **Chapter 15,** Sonya finds Anatole's letter and is very upset. She and Natasha have an argument. In the end, Natasha actually writes a letter to Marya to say that the engagement with Andrei is officially off.

Anatole is planning his "ruining" or Natasha (having sex with her before marriage and then dumping her) with his friend Dolokhov in **Chapter 16**. They are going to find a fake priest to pretend to marry them. When the two guys go to the house Natasha is staying at in **Chapter 17**, but a giant footman blocks their way, prompting them to run away.

In **Chapter 18**, we learn that Marya Dmitrievna learned from Sonya what was happening. She yelled at Natasha, locked her in her room, and protected her from Anatole. Natasha is so distraught that she's practically catatonic. Pierre comes over in **Chapter 19**, and he finds out what's been going on. He also reveals to Natasha that Anatole was never planning to marry her, since he was previously married.

Pierre is very upset with Anatole's actions in **Chapter 20.** He goes to his wife's house (where a party is happening) and finds his brother-in-law and pulls him into a private room. Pierre threatens Anatole and says he must leave Moscow. Pierre leaves the next day for Petersburg.

Andrei comes back in **Chapter 21**. He seems very cool about the situation with Natasha. When Pierre talks to him about it, pressing him for a response, Andrei reveals that he will never forgive Natasha. In **Chapter 22**, Pierre goes back and tells Natasha and her family how Andrei took everything. Natasha is very remorseful and upset, and Pierre is very touched by this. When he rides away, he has tears in his eyes. He sees the famous 1812 comet and is filled with hope.

BOOK IX

This book (or part, depending on what translation you're reading) begins by giving us an overview of the events surrounding the start of the War of 1812, between Russia and France. **Chapter 1** gives us some open narrative and commentary. Tolstoy tells us that war is useless and that there is often no obvious cause for history's wars.

Chapter 2 gives us more detail. We jump to May 29, 1812. Napoleon moves out east from Dresden. He crosses the Niemen River with his army, even though peace talks are still going on. When Napoleon gets to the Vilia River, he instructs some Polish troops to find a shallow place to cross. The men are so determined to impress the French Emperor, they just ride in and try to swim. They all drown, and Napoleon has the men receive a medal for their courage.

Meanwhile, in **Chapter 3,** we see that the Russian army is divided between three generals, and no one is really preparing for the French invasion that is obviously coming. Alexander is not happy about this. He writes a letter to Napoleon and sends it to the French. In **Chapter 4,** we see Alexander giving the letter to a man named Balashov to deliver to Napoleon. When he reaches the French, he gets passed around to French officials. He sees Murat, who is supposed to be King of Naples. After a little talk, Balashov gets sent to Marshal Davout. Time passes in **Chapter 5**, and finally Balashov goes to see Napoleon in person. All this time, while Balashov is getting passes around, the French has been moving further east. When Balashov actually meets Napoleon in **Chapter 6**, but he quickly sees that Napoleon has no intention of making peace. In **Chapter 7**, Balashov gets invited to dinner with Napoleon. The French ruler is pretending to be all nice and polite, asking about Russia like a tourist planning a visit. He shows affection by pulling on Balashov's ear. When Balashov ges back to Alexander, he describe everything that happened. The war officially begins.

In **Chapter 8,** Andrei goes looking for Anatole, hoping to get revenge for what went on with Natasha by forcing Anatole to duel. Anatole, though, is nowhere to be seen, because he's run off to join the army. Andrei also joins the army again, at first under Kutuzov (the same general he served under before) and later under another General named Barclay do Tolly. Along the way to joining the new general, Andrei stops home to visit his family. When he yells at his father to defend his sister, Marya, his father kicks him out of the house.

In **Chapter 9,** Andrei arrives with the army of de Tolly, who doesn't really know what to do with Andrei. Andrei quickly sees that the army is in chaos. There are several groups competing for control. Some want to attack, others want to retreat into Russia, and still others was to broker peace with the French. Alexander is convinced to leave the army and go on a morale-boosting tour through the country. Before Alexander leaves, he invites Andrei to dinner in **Chapters 10 and 11.** It seems that Alexander has invited several people to get a variety of opinion about how to win the war. They all just start arguing. This one guy, Pfuel, is very convinced that his is the best strategy, but he keeps getting overpowered. In the end, Andrei decides to just go back into the army to fight, disappointed by the chaos in the leadership.

Meanwhile, in **Chapter 12**, Nikolai gets a letter from his family and finds out that the marriage is off. He's asked to come home, but he's a captain in the army now, and he can't just leave. When Nikolai gets annoyed listening to exaggerated war stories, he goes to a tavern in **Chapter 13**. There, a doctor and his young, pretty wife. The wife gets teased by the soldiers in the tavern, until the doctor gets angry and leaves with her. The soldiers laugh themselves to sleep. In **Chapters 14 and 15,** they are all woken up in the middle of the night. The army is marching out again, this time right into battle. They line up, hearing the fighting ahead of them. They receive the call to attack, and Nikolai is excited. The men in front of him ride into battle, the sound of pellets in the air, but they immediately ride back. Nikolai sees that the retreating men are being pursued by French dragoons. When he sees an opportunity to attack them, he calls his men and leads an attack. They fight the French off, and Nikolai manages to take a prisoner. But almost killing the French man really disturbs him.

In **Chapter 16**, we see Natasha is super sick in Moscow, though the cause of the sickness is really mental and emotional. Doctors come to see her, and she seems to respond to the attention a little. In **Chapter 17**, Natasha seems to be doing better. She's spending more time with Pierre, who has romantic feelings for her but says nothing about it. Natasha also starts going to church more, which her mom thinks is a good sign. In **Chapter 18,** War is coming to Moscow, and everyone is nervous about it. Natasha is hurt when people start to gossip about her scandal with Anatole. She also gets upset when the priest prays for the Russian troops, basically wanting them to kill as many French as possible.

In **Chapter 19**, Pierre is completely falling for Natasha. He can't stop thinking about her. Pierre also starts playing around with numerology, looking for significance in numbers. He converts Napoleon to numbers and discovers that his name equals 666. He also plays around with his own name enough and gets 666, too. Pierre tells the Rostovs that Nikolai was promoted for taking a prisoner. Pierre goes to the Rostov's house and talks to Natasha in **Chapter 20**. She asks if he thinks Andrei will ever forgive her. Petya interrupts the conversation to ask about the military. Who they take him? Pierre says that they're taking anyone they can get at this point. Over dinner, Petya announces that he want to join the army, at which point their parents starts to freak out. When Pierre leaves their house, he decides not to visit the Rostov's anymore, because he's fallen too in love with Natasha.

Petya is very upset after that dinner. In **Chapter 21,** he cries himself to sleep. The next day, he gets ready to go out and meet Alexander, who will be visiting Moscow. (He's on the morale-boosting tour, remember?) He imagines going straight up to the tsar, or one of his personal ministers, and volunteering. When he does go out, he's very disappointed, since the streets are completely packed with people. Petya ends up barely even seeing Alexander. At one point, he's even knocked out by someone in the crowd, only to be protected by a church official.

Petya goes home and tells his parents that if they don't let him join the army, he'll run away and join anyway. So his father goes to find a place in the military for his son where it won't be too dangerous.

Book IX concludes with Pierre sitting in on this counsel, talking about how to better prepare and supply the troops. When Alexander comes in and thanks the all for their work, Pierre is overcome with tears.

BOOK X

Tolstoy gives us some more commentary on the ways of war in **Chapter 1**. Tolstoy sees that war is chaos, something that history often covers up. The French are doomed to lose the war, not because the Russians are stronger, but because the French are not prepared to endure a cold winter. Napoleon ignores this, pushes ahead for the capital.

In **Chapters 2 and 3,** we zoom in to the Bolkonsky's house again. After the Prince kicked Andrei out of the house, he took his frustration out on Marya. Later, Andrei sends a message to his father, apologizing. Andrei also tells them they must leave the area, since the war is coming close to Bleak Hills. The Prince doesn't believe this, and he send his servant to get supplies in Smolensk. We also see how confused and paranoid Prince Bolkonsky has gotten. The servant, Alpatych, travels to the town, in **Chapter 4,** where the fighting is currently very close. He delivers a letter and visits the inn. While he's arranging for the supplies, the French bombard the town. People start to dies around Alpatych, and others are setting fire to their buildings. Alpatych sees Andrei in the chaos, and he starts to cry to him. Andrei starts making a note to give to his sister Marya. He desperately wants the Bolkonskys to leave for Moscow.

In **Chapter 5,** the Russians continue to retreat, and the French continue to follow. They get very close to Bleak Hills, so Andrei rides out to make sure his family is gone. They are, and Andrei goes back to where his troops are. They are close to a pond, and it is so hot, Andrei wants to bathe in that dirty, nasty pond…until he sees how many men are already in the pond.

In **Chapter 6,** we see that Anna Pavlovna and Helene are still in Petersburg and having regular parties at their houses. In one house, the conversations are always against the French, and in the other house, the guests are French apologists. Prince Vassily goes back and forth to both parties, and he even starts to get confused and says things in the wrong party.

In **Chapter 7,** Napoleon keeps chasing the Russians, and the Russians manage to avoid any major battles, until they get to Borodino, 75 miles away from Moscow. Napoleon captures a Russian prisoner, who is interrogated and gives up that the French should attack sooner rather than later.

We see what happened with Marya and Andrei's family in **Chapter 8.** When Alpatych came back and delivered the instructions from Andrei, Prince Bolkonsky didn't listen. He was interested in defending the estate. When the Prince suffers from a stroke, Marya begins making plans to leave. By the time she gets back, the Prince has died from another stroke. In **Chapter 9**, we see that the Bolkonsky's serfs are not cooperating. They want to stay around and join the French. They won't even supply the horses and wagons for their master to leave. In **Chapter 10**, Marya makes peace with Mlle. Bourienne. But she continues to have trouble with the servants. She orders to have all the stored grain distributed to the serfs. In **Chapters 11 and 12,** Marya actually goes out and talks to the serfs. They don't want the grain. They want to stay and wait for the French and be free. Marya goes back inside and, again, orders the horses and wagons prepared. Marya spends the night in her room, feeling sad about her dad dying.

In **Chapters 13 and 14,** Nikolai rides out to the Bolkonsky's estate. When he learns about the problem, he promises to help take care of it so Marya and the others can get some horses and leave. He rides into where the serfs are and scares them into giving up some horses and a wagon. Marya thanks Nikolai, and his looking into her eyes makes him feel like he's in love with her. He even rides out with her to make sure they're okay. She also falls in love with him, thinking she'll probably never see him again.

In **Chapters 15 and 16,** Andrei is waiting to talk to Kutuzov when he runs into Denisov. They talk about Andrei's father's death. Kutuzov rides up and also expresses sadness over the late Prince Bolkonsky. Denisov has a plan to cut off the French's communications, but Kutuzov doesn't go for it. Kutuzov wants Andrei to stay with him as a counselor, but Andrei insists on being in the regiment and fighting with the other soldiers. Kutuzov's plan is to be patient.

Meanwhile, in **Chapter 17,** we zoom back to Moscow. The French are getting closer. Julie (Boris' wife) has a party at her house. They mock Pierre because he's going off to war, even though he's gotten pretty fat. They're also talking about Nikolai's saving Marya like a knight in shining armor. Also shuffled into the gossip is the Natasha-Andrei-Anatole scandal. Pierre rides home in **Chapter 18.** He's beginning to worry. He's scared and strangely determined when he sees a man being publicly whipped for suspicion for being a French spy.

Chapter 19 gives us an overview of how the battle of Borodino gets set up. The location and timing of the battle is unwise for both sides. Nothing is properly organized, and both sides are set up to lose a lot of troops. Pierre rides into the battle area in **Chapters 20 and 21,** seeing some soldiers already mutilated and bloody. He sees all the soldiers just waiting to fight, and he realizes that soon most of these boys will be dead. He looks over the future battlefield. A sacred image is being carried around, and soldiers are kneeling before it for a blessing.

In **Chapter 22,** Pierre is invited by both Kutuzov and another General named Bennigsen to ride with them to see the fighting. Pierre decides to take Bennigsen up on his offer. In **Chapter 23,** Bennigsen moves some soldier from the underside of a hill to the top, not knowing that this was a strategy to ambush the enemy.

Andrei is in his shed in **Chapters 24 and 25,** waiting for the fighting to begin. He's thinking about how he might die tomorrow, so he starts feeling sorry for himself. Pierre comes with him, and Andrei invites Timokhin to join the two of them for tea. They talk about the upcoming battle, the strategy, and the generals leading everything. Andrei goes to be that night thinking about Natasha.

On the French side, which we see in **Chapters 26 and 27**, Napoleon is trying hard to look like a good leader. He has a portrait of his son, but, after looking at it with fatherly affection, he has it taken down, so his "son" won't see the battle. Napoleon also starts riding around giving orders to his men, looking very official, even though his orders are confusing and superficial.

In **Chapter 28**, Tolstoy takes a very cynical view of the battle of Borodino. Who won? What was the point of it all? The chaos of battle and the endless killing turned out to be overwhelming compared to the actual planning and strategy.

Napoleon continues to give orders in **Chapter 29**. After dinner, he plans to rest early, in preparation for the next day's battle. Instead of going to bed, he goes for a walk, chatting with soldiers along the way. He ends up going for a ride, and, before he realizes it, shots are being fired. The battle has begun.

Meanwhile, in **Chapter 30**, Pierre is at Andrei's house. He wakes up late to the distant sounds of battle. He looks at the battlefield and sees it as beautiful, full of people running around, sounds of bullets and cannons in the air. Pierre rides down into the battlefield with a general. In **Chapters 31 and 32**, Pierre loses the general and ends up in the way. A soldier volunteers to take him to a better place where he can watch the action and not be in the way. He sees people and horses dying all around him. Pierre tries to run away from the scene, and faces a French soldier. He and the soldier grab each other, and Pierre ends up letting the guy go. Some Russian soldiers run up later and kill the French soldier.

In **Chapters 33 and 34,** Napoleon is far away from the battle, receiving reports and giving orders. But his orders are usually out of date before they leave his tent. Napoleon keeps getting requests for reinforcements, and he keeps saying no. When he finally rides out to see the battle himself, he sees all the carnage and chaos, and he sees that he's been defeated.

In **Chapter 35,** Kutuzov is in his tent, listening to reports. But he isn't giving many orders. He mostly listens, trying to get the basic idea of how the battle is going. Everything seems to wind down by mid afternoon, and it seems the Russians have won. Except, at dinner that evening, one counselor says the French have won. Kutuzov responds by sending out word that tomorrow the Russians will attack the already decimated French.

In **Chapter 36,** Andrei is instructed to stand around with his regiment of reserves. The men keep dying from stray bullets or cannon fire. A grenade lands on the ground nearby. Out of a sense of honor, Andrei refuses to duck down. He just stands there when the grenade blows, and he's blown back and lands, blood gushing from his body. He ends up on a stretcher and in the hospital. He fears he's going to die, and he mourns the parts of his life he never figured out. In **Chapter 37**, Andrei gets immediate attention. He passes out from the pain of the operation. He wakes up to find Anatole crying over him. Andrei decides in that moment that he's willing to forgive Anatole for the whole Natasha scandal.

Meanwhile, in **Chapter 38,** Napoleon is standing over the battlefield, disgusted by the carnage. He's told that the guns firing on the Russians are doing very much damage. He says they need to fire more. In **Chapter 39,** the battle finally just fade out, everyone too exhausted to continue.

BOOK XI

In **Chapter 1**, Tolstoy argues that analyzing a war is futile, since it doesn't make sense. He looks at it from different points of view, like different kinds of math. This mathematical theory stuff is applied to the War of 1812 in **Chapter 2**. The French push forward, which eventually leads to their demise. The Russians retreat, but not on purpose. After the major battle of Borodino, the Russians retreat passed Moscow, allowing the French to take the city. In **Chapters 3 and 4**, we see the Russian try to strategize to make losing Moscow a good thing. They want to retake it. Kutuzov say that they need to let the French have the city. The announcement is made; Moscow is to be abandoned. In **Chapter 5**, Napoleon gets to Moscow. News gets out about the brave residents of the city that burned it down instead of allowing the French to move in. Tolstoy says this isn't completely correct; most of the fires are the accidental effect of an empty city with wooden buildings.

Helene runs into an interesting problem in **Chapters 6 and 7.** She's been seeing two men. Now they've both come back to her after the war, and Helene doesn't know which one to choose. She says she'll stay with the one that marries her first. They also have to get a divorce from Pierre for her. Some people react badly to this, but her father, Prince Vassily, is very supportive. Meanwhile, Pierre gets a letter asking him for a divorce.

In **Chapters 8 and 9**, Pierre runs from the wake of the battle, trying to get as far away from the horrible mess as possible. He walks along a road until he gets tire, and then he lays on the ground and sleeps. He gets up and continues on. He ends up sleeping in his carriage because the nearby inns are full. He has some very strange dreams while he sleeps. When he wakes up, he hears that Andrei is dead. In **Chapter 10,** Pierre gets back to Moscow and visits the Governor. He discovers that the Governor is distributing propaganda that the citizens must defend the city instead of leave. When he meets with the Governor in **Chapter 11,** Pierre is bombarded with questions about him being a Mason. It seems that the Masons are accused of being traitors. Pierre is told to leave town and not have any more dealings with the Masons. He's upset when he gets home, and the problems multiply when he gets that letter from Helene, asking for a divorce.

In **Chapter 12,** the Rostovs are still in Moscow, even though everyone else is evacuating as fast as possible. The Countess is freaking out and trying to pack. Even when it's the day before the French comes, they are still there. Petya comes back, and he and Natasha aren't really helping with the packing. In **Chapter 13,** Natasha invites some wounded soldiers to stay in the house. That night at dinner, Petya says that the Governor is handing out weapons to the city's residents. His parents don't like hearing this, fearing that Petya's going to run off and join the fight. Packing continues in **Chapter 14,** and Natasha starts helping more. Meanwhile, a new wounded soldier arrives, and Natasha discovers that it's Andrei, still alive!

In **Chapter 15,** it's the last day before the French take Moscow. A militia gathers to defend the city, but they're doomed to fail, especially when their fearless Governor doesn't even show up. The militia goes off to get drunk instead of fight. Count Rostov wants to unload a few wagons to make room for some wounded officers, but the Countess doesn't want to give anything up. In **Chapter 16,** Berg comes to visit the Rostovs. He asks for money, of all things. Natasha gets upset when the officers are not getting on the wagons, and she goes to yell at her mom for being greedy. Natasha goes back outside and gets the wounded onto the wagons. When all the carts are ready to go in **Chapter 17**, Sonya realizes that one of the wounded is Andrei, but they decide not to tell Natasha. On the way out of the city, they spot Pierre, who seems confused and distracted.

In **Chapter 18,** we see what Pierre's been doing. He's been walking around in a daze, and he even went and got a gun.

Napoleon stands on a hill and looks over the city or Moscow in **Chapters 19 and 20.** He talks about how glorious the city looks, and he's waiting for the Russian delegation. He has this plan, saying that there won't be any pillaging or looting. They're going to be civil to the Russian. What he doesn't know is the Russians are gone and there isn't any Russian delegation coming. As he makes his way into the city, he discovers that the city is nearly empty, and he's not happy about it because his dramatic moment is lost.

In **Chapter 21,** we see how Moscow's bridges are crowded with people trying to get out. Some Russian soldiers do some looting along the way. One general actually pretends he's about to shoot the crowd with a cannon.

In **Chapter 22,** the Rostov house is nearly deserted. Only some housekeepers are around. Someone comes begging for money, and the housekeeper gives him 25 rubles.

In **Chapter 23**, a mob forms. At first, there is a fight between factory workers and blacksmiths, but when a man is almost killed, the group makes its way to the Governor's office, and the mob swells as it goes along. Meanwhile, in **Chapter24**, the Governor is upset because he'd being instructed to leave Moscow. He wasn't even invited to Kutuzov's war council. He walks out onto his porch in **Chapter 25,** just in time to meet the swelling mob, now calling themselves a freedom militia. The governor has the prisons opened, but he has a political prisoner. He orders mob to kill the young man, saying he's the one responsible for the downfall of Moscow. The crowd takes the man and beat him until he dies.

The French come into the city in **Chapter 26.** They expect a fight at first, but there isn't much of anyone around. They move into the Kremlin and surrounding houses. The soldiers start to loot the place, and soon the city is on fire. Some will later say that the French did this on purpose, and others will say that the Russians did it to not allow the French to take the city. Tolstoy says that the fires were simply the result of an empty city with wooden buildings. No one was around to take care of things, so fires spread quickly.

Pierre has been losing his mind for the past two days. As we see in **Chapter 27,** he's been reading Mason books and thinking about numerology. He remembers that his name (through some serious manipulation) comes to 666, just like Napoleon. He figures this means he must kill Napoleon. While he's planning to do this, though, someone steals his gun. He goes looking for the guy who stole his gun. When a French officer comes to Pierre's house in **Chapter 28,** wanting to stay there. The guy who had stolen Pierre's gun jumps out and tries to shoot the French officer. Pierre saves his life. The officer and Pierre become friends now, the officer demands food and wine so they can eat together. In **Chapter 29**, they have dinner together and talk a lot, the wine helping loosen the jaws.

In **Chapters 30 and 31,** the Rostovs are moving away from town. They see the fires, and the dry weather could make them spread even more. Sonya and her mom start to cry out of fear, in fact. Natasha, now having been told that Andrei is one of the wounded officers traveling with them, doesn't seem to care about the fires. When they find a place to sleep for the night, Natasha sneaks over to where Andrei is. When she sees him, he wakes up, smiles and giver her his hand.

In **Chapter 32,** we see how Andrei and Natasha come together again, sort of. He's eating and drinking a little, which surprises the doctors, but he's also hallucinating. He keeps going back to that moment when he sees Anatole crying beside him, leg amputated. He remembers the love the felt then. Now Natasha stays with him day and night. Everyone still assumes that Andrei will die soon.

In **Chapters 33 and 34,** Pierre wakes up and is ready to kill Napoleon. He's on his way to find the French ruler, but he manages to save a child from a fire along the way. He then tries to save another girl from being raped by a French soldier. He's arrested for being a Russian rebel and locked in a house, under guard.

BOOK XII

In **Chapter 1,** we jump to Petersburg just before the battle of Borodino. Everyone is gossiping about Helene, who is apparently sick and seeing some new doctor from Spain. In **Chapter 2,** everyone is happy about a letter from Kutuzov, announcing the Russian victory in Borodino. That happy news is forgotten when everyone hears the Helene has died. The official story is that she had a heart illness. But the rumors say that she was pregnant, using a hot-shot Spanish doctor to induce a miscarriage. When Pierre never answered her written request for a divorce, she apparently overdosed on meds and killed herself.

In **Chapter 3**, Kutuzov sends a message to Alexander, breaking the news about the abandoning of Moscow. Alexander tells everyone that's listening that is he stops being emperor, he'll be a peasant and eat potatoes.

In **Chapter 4,** Nikolai is sent ahead of his division of the army to get new supplies. He has some free time, so he goes to a ball and talks to some of the important people from the town. In **Chapter 5,** he's flirting with another man's wife. She tells him that Marya is in town. Everyone knows how he rode in and save her. Nikolai doesn't know what to do. He has feelings for Marya, but he's already promised to marry Sonya.

In **Chapter 6,** Marya and Nikolai get to talk, and they both really fall for each other. In **Chapter 7,** when word of Borodino makes it to the town. Nikolai goes to the church service in honor of the Russian victory, and he sees Marya there. Now Nikolai is in trouble, because he's so in love with Marya, but he's promised for Sonya. Just in time, he gets a letter from Sonya, saying that he's now free from his promise of marriage. The letter also says that Andrei is with Natasha and the Rostovs. Nikolai tells Marya, and she goes off to find them.

In **Chapter 8,** Sonya's life is very hard right now. Remember, the Countess, Nikolai's mom, doesn't want Nikolai and Sonya getting married because Sonya doesn't have any money. She makes Sonya feel guilty about tying Nikolai down, preventing him from marrying Marya. Sonya sends that letter, letting Nikolai off the hook, because she figures that Andrei will get better and marry Natasha, making Marya and Nikolai's relationship awkward.

In **Chapters 9 and 10,** Pierre has been spending a lot of time in prison. He's been refusing to give up any information about himself, so he's taken to a general for some firmer interrogation. This general looks Pierre in the eyes and asks him questions. Pierre just looks back, and the two men make some kind of deep, human connection. Nonetheless, Pierre discovers he has been sentenced to death. In **Chapter 11,** Pierre is taken out of where he's being held with a bunch of other prisoners. They are lined up, and the French soldiers start shooting them in pairs. Pierre is number 6. Surprisingly, he is not shot. He and a few others have been spared.

In **Chapters 12 and 13,** Pierre and the others that were spared are taken to some POW barracks. There, Pierre just feels completely lost and without any faith. He meets a man in the barracks named Platon. After talking to this Platon, Pierre feels a little of his faith coming back. Pierre and Platon continue to talk for the next weeks. Platon is a round man, full of energy. Pierre knows right off that he'll never forget him.

In **Chapter 14**, we see Marya going off to the city were the Rostovs and Andrei are. She is both happy about talking to Nikolai again, she is also stressed about her brother, Andrei. She finds the Rostovs' house. She demands to see Andrei, but the countess is dragging her feet. Finally, Natasha comes in, and they cry together. Marya knows Andrei won't make it very long.

In **Chapters 15 and 16,** we find out that Andrei gave up on living two days ago. He and Marya meet and talk. But Andrei has already decided that he to die is to be one with God and love. He desires to let go of life and join all that love, like the love he felt when Anatole was crying by him in the hospital. Finally, Andrei dies. Everyone cries over him.

BOOK XIII

Again, in **Chapter 1,** we see an overview of the causes of the battle of Borodino. Tolstoy shows that no one event or person could have caused or predicted what happened. The Russians retreated south, to more supplied cities. This turned out to be a good move, but Tolstoy says is was just blind luck. Napoleon sends a letter to Kutuzov in **Chapter 2.** The French ruler wants to wrap things up, which probable means he expects the Russians to surrender. Kutuzov ignores the proposal. Meanwhile, the Russians are getting stronger while the French are getting weaker.

In **Chapter 3,** Alexander is writing Kutuzov, wondering why the Russians aren't attack the French. But by the time the letter gets to Kutuzov, there's already been a battle. The battle of Tarutino started by accident, when a Russian soldier runs into some French soldier while on patrol. News spreads, and everyone itching for a fight just runs out and does so. A battle results.

There is this funny scene in **Chapter 4,** in which a messenger is sent to find General Ermolov, but he can't find the man. When the messenger finally finds the general, it turns out the general was hiding, avoiding order to make his superior look bad. When Kutuzov heads out to see the battle in **Chapter 5**, he discovers that no one has attacked. He yells at his generals, who apologize and say they'll attack the next day. So, in **Chapter 6**, the next day, the army is a little more with the program. A French deserter comes and say he can lead the Russians to Murat (the French general). They send one hundred men out with him, but later they command them to come back, thinking it may be trap. Instead, they decide to attack full force.

In **Chapter 7,** we see just how much of a mess the battle of Tarutino is. Even though no objectives are met on the Russian side, the battle does change things, putting the French on the defensive and on the run.

Tolstoy criticizes Napoleon in **Chapter 8.** The French ruler did not prevent his men from looting Moscow. They could have preserved the city and combed it for suppolies, like food and warm clothing. Then, he could have marched on Petersburg and finished off the Russians. In **Chapters 9 and 10**, we see what Napoleon does do and how it doesn't work. He send Murat to find out where Kutuzov and the Russian army went, but Murat never find him. He sends messengers to Alexander to broker peace, but the messenger never makes it. He also fails to stop Moscow from burning down. After the battle of Tarutino, they panic and flee Moscow, a long train of wagons loaded with stuff from Moscow. Napoleon, Tolstoy says Napoleon is being lead by his army at this point instead of being the leader.

In **Chapter 11,** we look back in on Pierre, still friends with Platon. Platon sews something for a French soldier, and the soldier leaves the scraps of cloth so he can make some socks for himself. In **Chapter 12,** we see how great Pierre feels, even though he's been in prison. Now he feels like he's ready for anything. In **Chapters 13 and 14,** Pierre and the other prisoners are marched out of Moscow with the French. They see some horrors of the city, and they're treated badly by the French. After gruel for dinner, Pierre still goes to sleep happy.

In **Chapter 15,** a small group of Russian soldiers goes out to the town of Fominskoe. They're expecting a small group of French soldiers, but they're surprised to find the entire French army, Napoleon included. An envoy is sent back to the generals for orders. In **Chapters 16 and 17,** the envoy arrives and word is sent to Kutuzov, who has been worried about the validity of Russia's supposed victory over the French. When he hears that the French army is so small an all in one place, he is so happy, he actually starts to cry.

In **Chapters 18 and 19,** Kutuzov holds the Russians back as long as he can. Meanwhile, the French army is losing men left and right. Napoleon is almost captured by Russian soldiers that run right into the middle of the French army and loot the wagons of booty. Finally, the Russians can't be stopped, and many French just up and leave, the rest of the army is on the run.

BOOK IV

In **Chapter 1,** Tolstoy challenges the rules of warfare. Normally, when an army beats another one, the losing country must submit to the victor. But this doesn't really make sense, since even a giant army represents only a tiny fraction of the nation's overall resources. Kutuzov also challenges these rules. Even though Russia actually retreated from the battle of Borodino, the French army's numbers were so devastated, they eventually had to leave, being overrun by the Russians.

In **Chapter 2,** Tolstoy shows that another winning strategy of the Russians was Guerrilla warfare, in which civilians and ex-soldiers attack the edges of the French armies. In **Chapter 3,** we see that Denisov is working in one of such guerrilla groups. They're planning a major attack, and they capture a French drummer boy to get some intel. But the boy is too scared to talk. In **Chapter 4,** Petya comes riding up with a letter from a nearby general. He's very happy to see Denisov, and he asks if he can stay with him.

In **Chapters 5 and 6,** Denisov rides out to investigate what the French are doing. A Russian scout comes back, bit without any prisoners. Denisov isn't very happy about that. But the scout did manage to get enough intel to plan an attack.

In **Chapter 7,** Petya is begging Denisov to let him be part of the raid they're planning. He shares all his supplies to show how cool he is. He also gives food to the French drummer boy. When Dolokhov walks in, in **Chapter 8,** Petya is in shock. Dolokhov wants to dress up as a French soldier and sneak into the camp, in order to get more intel before they go out and attack. Petya volunteers to go with him.

In **Chapter 9,** the two of them go into the camp, getting passed the guards. Even when some French soldiers are suspicious, Dolokhov plays it cool and gets in. Petya is very excited about it. They come back to the Russian camp in **Chapter 10**. Petya is super excited about fighting the next day.

When they do ride out for the raid in **Chapter 11,** Petya rides ahead of everyone else and is immediately shot in the head. Denisov is so struck by this that he gets physically ill. The good news: they manage to free some Russian prisoners, including Pierre.

We see Pierre's story in **Chapters 12, 13, and 14.**
The prisoners have been marching all along, and
they've been getting killed from the guerrilla attacks
along with French soldiers. Along the way, Pierre
tries to focus on the positive. Meanwhile, Platon is
getting sick. He talks to Platon one last time, but
when the soldiers line the prisoners up and there is
come talk about Platon, the old man ends up getting
shot. Pierre turns away, refusing to look. Pierre goes
to sleep in **Chapter 15,** but has troublesome dreams.
When he wakes up, Dolokhov and his men are raiding
the place, freeing Pierre and taking almost two
hundred French prisoners.

In **Chapters 16 and 17,** it's a week later and the
weather's getting colder. The French army is
suffering. As the French army retreats, the Russians
chase after them. Napoleon leads the escape, not
caring if all the French army survives behind him.
Tolstoy takes **Chapter 18** to talk about how bad a
leader Napoleon is.

Chapter 19 is Tolstoy's explanation about why the
entire French army isn't wiped out. Because they
aren't a unified mass. They're just small groups of
men rushing to get out of the country, as the intense
winter freezes them and kills them off.

BOOK XV

In **Chapter 1**, Natasha shuts down after Andrei's death. She just stares into space and has imaginary conversations with him. To make things worse, a letter arrives about Petya. The news of Petya's death tears the family up in **Chapter 2.** The countess loses her sanity and slips into denial. Natasha has to stay with her. In **Chapter 3,** Marya was planning to leave the Rostovs, but now she stays around to take care of Natasha, who, in turn, has to take care of her mother. Natasha and Marya grow closer.

In **Chapter 4**, we pull back and get an overview of the war. The Russian army is in sore straights, but near as sore as the French. They continue to follow after the French, against Kutuzov's will. Every time the two armies meet in the field, the French are slaughtered easily, important officers taken prisoner. We see how Kutuzov was remembered by history in **Chapter 5**: as an old buffoon. Tolstoy sees things differently. To him, Kutuzov was a wise man that made excellent decisions. He understood both the chaos of war and the true wishes of the Russian people.

In **Chapters 6 and 7,** we see one of the battles between the French and the Russians. It's a slaughter, and prisoners are taken afterward. Kutuzov gives a speech to the men, thanking them for their service and saying some derogatory things about Napoleon. The men laugh and cheer at that. After that, the soldiers clean up part of the battlefield and set up camp, laughing and sweating the whole time. In **Chapter 8,** some of the Russian soldiers warm up by a campfire, telling war stories and ghost tales about the French. They hear a noise in the bushes in **Chapter 9.** It turns out it's Ramballe, the same French officer that Pierre met in Moscow before the war. (Pierre saved his life, remember?) The Russians feed and help the French soldiers with Ramballe. They even sing songs with them.

The French are still on the run in **Chapters 10 and 11.** The Russian generals cut them off and attack. The French don't surrender and just keep running into some freezing water, trying to get to a boat there. Kutuzov is becoming less popular in his ideas, since he doesn't want the Russians to chase the French anymore. Alexander actually sends him a letter, basically saying to step down. Kutuzov leaves military life, but he's also given a very high medal from Alexander himself. It turns out the medal (called the Order of St. George) is just a formality. Kutuzov doesn't allow this formality to stop him from giving his opinion, just now nobody listens.

In **Chapter 12,** we see how Pierre reacts to learning that both Andrei and Petya being dead. Despite what has happened, despite what he's personally been through, Pierre feels free and at peace. In **Chapter 13,** Pierre takes control of his life. He makes financial decisions and helps others in cool ways. He goes off to Moscow.

In **Chapter 14,** Tolstoy describes how Moscow slowly gets rebuilt. First the looters get back, but the more looters there are, the more things start to get organized. Soon, officials, artists, homeowners, and carpenters arrive. Order is eventually restored, and it's business as usual.

Pierre returns to Moscow in **Chapter 15.** He starts living in a wing of his house there. He goes to visit Marya, who came with Natasha earlier. When he sees Marya, they talk about Andrei, when he sees that the person with Marya is Natasha (which he doesn't at first because she is so thin and pale), he realizes all over again that he is still madly in love with her. In **Chapter 16,** Pierre and Natasha talk about Petya. Natasha talks about how she took care of Andrei. She ends up having to leave the room. Andrei's son comes in to say hi to Pierre.

In **Chapter 17**, Pierre, Natasha, and Marya continue talking, though it's a little awkward for everyone. Pierre's singleness comes up, and Marya realizes that Natasha and Pierre really like each other. When Pierre leaves, they talk about how wonderful Pierre is.

Meanwhile, Pierre goes home in **Chapter 18,** deciding to marry Natasha. Even when he looks at the ruins of Moscow, he sees beauty. He goes to dinner at Marya's place and asks her for help in convincing Natasha to marry him. She tells him to wait. He has to leave anyway on a business trip, and Natasha tells him she'll be waiting for him. Pierre is so happy and in love, it's as if he's floating on air in **Chapter 19.** Meanwhile, in **Chapter 20,** Natasha is becoming her old self again, smiling and happy. She hasn't forgotten Andrei, or course, but she's obviously in love with Pierre.

FIRST EPILOGUE

In **Chapter 1,** Tolstoy talks about Alexander's political career. Alexander started out very liberal, but ended up very reactionary (which just means no forward advancement). Some people hate him for that, but Tolstoy not so much. In **Chapter 2,** Tolstoy continues to talk about how historians are wrong. While historians look for either random chance or personal genius to explain events, Tolstoy looks for some higher power at work. In **Chapters 3 and 4,** Tolstoy sums up Napoleon's military career and the War of 1812 as a big coincidence. Napoleon, according to Tolstoy was simply in the right place at the right time; he wasn't any kind of military genius. Power flows through people. It flowed through Napoleon and made him the most powerful person on earth, and then Alexander became the most powerful. We don't know why things happen. They just do.

In **Chapter 5,** we leave the philosophy for a while and get back to the characters we know and love. Pierre and Natasha get married in 1813. Count Rostov (Natasha's father) dies happy, knowing his daughter found love. Nikolai comes home after that. Things are bad for the family, financially and otherwise, but Nikolai dedicates himself to taking care of his mother and Sonya. In **Chapters 6 and 7,** Marya visits the Rostovs, but Nikolai is not nice to her. He kind of ignores her. He's forced by his mother to visit them back, but he's cold to Marya then, too. When he's about to leave, Marya demands why he won't open up to her. She gets the idea that Nikolai is embarrassed about being poor. He really still loves her, and she him, and they get marries a few months later. Nikolai manages to pay all the family's debts, and he even ends up enlarging the estate. He's so nice to his serfs and everyone starts to prosper. Word gets out that he's a great master, and nearby serfs beg to be purchased from their masters so they can work for Nikolai, too.

In **Chapter 8,** we see how Marya has a good effect on Nikolai. When she sees him beating a serf, she cries, which moves him to repentance. He starts being even nicer to his serfs. Instead of living a social life, he oversees his serfs at the farms and reads at night, eventually building up an extensive library.

In **Chapter 9,** we see the two couples later, in 1820. They all have kids. Natasha and her kids visit Nikolai and Marya. At first, Nikolai is moody. He snaps at Marya and goes to take a nap. Later, one of his kids wakes him up, and Nikolai gets mad at first, but then he calms down and gets happy. Just then, Pierre arrives, making Natasha happy.

In **Chapter 10,** we see how Natasha and Pierre's marriage is going. After getting married, they had four kids right away, and both Natasha and Pierre got very involved in taking care of family, so much so that they spent little time on social activities. In **Chapter 11,** we get back to the here and now. Pierre's been away for six weeks on business. Natasha is upset about him being gone for so long. Pierre is very sorry, and he goes to cuddle his baby in the nursery. When Nikolai walks in, he is grossed out by the baby. Marya explains that Nikolai hates babies. He only starts playing with his kids after they're a year old or so. Both women brag about what great dads their husbands are. In **Chapter 12,** Pierre gives everyone presents, and that makes everyone happy.

Pierre wants to tell everyone about the latest gossip from Petersburg in **Chapter 13,** but he can't because Countess Rostov is in the room. She's becoming more and more senile, and she doesn't remember anyone from Petersburg. She only wants to talk about the people she knew when she was young. When the Countess finally leaves in **Chapter 14**, the gossip starts and Pierre starts talking about how badly the government is going. He starts hinting that the best course of action is perhaps to oppose the government to change it. This make Nikolai angry, since he thinks that citizens should be loyal to their government no matter what. He's especially upset because Andrei's son is in the room, and such revolutionary talk is bad for children to hear.

In **Chapters 15 and 16,** Nikolai and Marya go to bed, and Marya shows her husband a diary she keeps about the kids and family. Nikolai realizes that she is such a great mom. Meanwhile, Natasha and Pierre also talk in their own little way. They even finish each others' sentences. They know they love each other, and Natasha sees that Pierre, the man she loves and knows as a husband, is also a political genius.

SECOND EPILOGUE

Since there is no characters or plot in this epilogue, we'll skip the chapter divisions and give a quick rundown. This entire epilogue is basically Tolstoy criticizing historians some more, since he apparently seed enough of that throughout the novel already.

Tolstoy says that historians try to do the impossible: record the happenings of an entire nation. Since this is impossible, the historians usually just follow the "great men" that lead these nations. Tolstoy goes on to question the idea of a nation having power.

On the other hand, there must be a connection between the commands of leaders and the movement of nations. Napoleon commands and an army invades Russia, for example. Napoleon caused that to happen. But, since commands take time to be carried out, and leaders are often in the middle of the events they are trying to change, their power is limited.

Tolstoy's debate then turns to the concept of free will. Do we make our decisions or is there some power over us? And can our reason limit our own will?

In all, Tolstoy questions and criticizes every form of historical study. He shows himself to not only be a writer of fiction, but also a deep think in search for truth in history.

About BookCaps

We all need refreshers every now and then. Whether you are a student trying to cram for that big final, or someone just trying to understand a book more, BookCaps can help. We are a small, but growing company, and are adding titles every month.

Visit www.bookcaps.com to see more of our books, or contact us with any questions.

45045648R00064

Made in the USA
San Bernardino, CA
30 January 2017